C000263568

ROBBERGIRLS

ALSO BY KADDY BENYON

POETRY
Milk Fever (2013)
The Tidal Wife (2018)

KADDY BENYON
Robbergirls

SALT

SHEFFIELD

PUBLISHED BY SALT PUBLISHING 2023

2 4 6 8 10 9 7 5 3 1

Copyright © Kaddy Benyon 2023

Kaddy Benyon has asserted her right under the Copyright, Designs and Patents Act 1988 to be identified as the author of this work.

This book is sold subject to the condition that it shall not, by way of trade or otherwise, be lent, resold, hired out, or otherwise circulated without the publisher's prior consent in any form of binding or cover other than that in which it is published and without a similar condition including this condition being imposed on the subsequent publisher.

First published in Great Britain in 2023 by
Salt Publishing Ltd
18 Churchill Road, Sheffield, S10 1FG United Kingdom

www.saltpublishing.com

Salt Publishing Limited Reg. No. 5293401

A CIP catalogue record for this book is available from the British Library

ISBN 978 1 78463 289 2 (Paperback edition)

Typeset in Sabon by Salt Publishing

Printed and bound in Great Britain by Clays Ltd, Elcograf S.p.A

MIX
Paper from
responsible sources
FSC® C018072

for Dad
(Paul Robert Benyon 1946–2003)

Then the flame died, the cigar glowed and filled the compartment with a remembered fragrance that made me think of my father, how he would hug me in a warm fug of Havana, when I was a little girl, before he kissed me and left me and died.

—ANGELA CARTER, *The Bloody Chamber*

Contents

ROBBERGIRLS

Prelude

Here she is: Gerda.
At the centre (not the edge) of a flooded meadow,
frozen marble-hard overnight.
The ice can hold her weight sure enough,
but remains unstable—not quite fixed—something pulsing
far below, blue-veined and involuntarily held.

A barn owl swoops low,
then lower than the sightline, landing-gear
down to snatch whatever sleeps there in deep time:
a toad, a shrew, a girl's untameable heart.
But—
she's moving too fast through this raw evening light,
in this place that never darkens,
sweat crystals spangling her lashes, her hair,
her lungs aflame with this breathless work of becoming
something other than her brother.

She's spinning herself into existence. Spinning
so fast she turns eight-armed and spiderlike: goddess
of destruction and creation, both. Hear her howl
as though surprised by joy; howl as though mad with it.
What shatters is not bone but moment.
The violence of a yawl skids her to to an ice-dust stop.
She teeters—landscape still wheeling—motion-sick
with feeling; there's nothing worse than a girl interrupted.
Oh Kai—idiot boy—what has he upended now?

PART ONE

either

THE MIRROR AND ITS FRAGMENTS

or

MIRROR

By seeking to read the riddle of his soul in its myriad manifestations, man is brought face to face with his own mysterious mirror image, an image which he confronts with mingled curiosity and fear.

—Sylvia Plath, *The Magic Mirror*

A Shattering

no sign of him   only myself in pieces   strewn
across   the flagstone floor   a thousand-bit jigsaw
glittering   lit   I now must reassemble
   it trembled   on the wall forever   trembled
to hold   that hinterland   between you and me
how to negotiate   ownership   of a space
   where we break   against one another   and reflection
falls off   before hitting   where each brief encounter
         is nothing but a loss   of holding
   it feels like   a kind of mourning   this putting back
together   when some of my parts   no longer   fit
   and I come back   disordered   and wrong   I long
   for a fairytale place   where mirrors talk back
instead of this iced   silence   that won't let me   know
   my own rage   perhaps   a broken moment
(all seven years bad luck)   is the best   time
      to quest   after your lost other   to gather
   yourself up   muffle the latch   and run Gerda
run   run hard   from this   surrendered dark

Mirror | Mirror

For mirror, read mother:
primitive, exacting, pernickety;
incapable of any good reflection when
so little passes between them—other than
her incapacity to attune her needs to Hans'.
So here he is, trapped between anguish and
desire; and wanting only to break free of
the frame; of this thing between them
that both silences and binds,
smothers and shames.
Sweet mother
of god
just
let
him
write
and
write
freely.

Portrait of a Lady on Ice

A cobbler and his son, peering through a wintered
window in a small yellow house in Odense.
Father is buffer between this son and a part-reflected mother

who bustles by the range: huffing, puffing, slamming
the cutlery drawer; tasting the same old fish stew as yesterday.
The son closes his eyes, traces a finger across knotty frost

as his father tells him of the cold lady: an ice maiden
who sweeps in hunting for lost boys and men,
blowing ice dust in their eyes and their hearts, before fetching

them away to her far north palace where she kisses
them all to death. The son's eyes widen as the tale lands hard
in the cold store of his mind set to germinate in the spring.

For now, he exhales his hot held breath on darkest glass
and watches as an opening grows into a peephole,
a portal, an enchanted doorway to escape this too-small place.

The Snow Queen

Whitely I will come for you.
In a night of whitest heat,
bed clothes roiling at your feet, I will come,

snatch you up in my furs, my skins,
a tangled knit of wintry limbs,
as I shapeshift from virgin to ermine—a deathly siren.

I will hush your blue-black lips,
run fingertips through your ice-stiff hair, hold
back your pulse, your hips,

whispering: promises, promises.
You'll forget to remember your dreams, your kin,
the rules of mathematics. You'll forget

the perfection of roses, snowflakes,
your grandmother's fireside tales. You'll forsake
all dreams and memories for kisses so bitter

they'll twist you to your knees. I'll quietly freeze
your pleading face in my cracked and wicked mirror,
before abandoning you: whitely, whitely.

Watching *The Storyteller* with Dad

When people told themselves their past with stories,
explained their present with stories, foretold the future with stories,
the best place by the fire was kept for the storyteller.
—ANTHONY MINGHELLA, *The Storyteller*

In the not-so-long ago, in the deep southeast
where I swore a cold, wicked heart ruled the land (my mother
had cuffed me for scuffing my new shoes, so naturally,
I despised her), back when I hadn't yet questioned why fairy
tale girls were so careless with their footwear,
or why all the wickedness is given to women. It was 1987,
and there was to be a royal wedding. My best friend

had just moved far, far away and I was beside myself
with missing her, missing all the things we used to do:
make dens, light fires, throw cackling shadows
onto walls through those dark rural Suffolk afternoons.
Since she'd left, I'd put myself into a kind of exile.
I tended to lean sleepy against my dad watching TV,
exhausted by hormones, undone homework—my giant

teenage feelings. I longed for a forest I was forbidden to visit,
dreamed of being an abandoned child who fell in with thieves
and bandits, who cut her teeth on filth and thuggery,
who needed somebody regal to see her true beauty
even through dirty, matted hair. I don't know if Dad saw
the importance of us watching those stories together,
stories where girls are tough and tender, touched and loved.

White on White

I

The aeronaut's photographer pans back, tiptoes along a crust of too-young ice, focused only on capturing the beast. Collapsed, greyscale, it deflates and rasps like a shot lung in dusty air as the hunters stake it, victorious. Andrée: staggering a thousand tangled miles from Danskøya to New Iceland; his face, a mirror of resolve, hot-veined Viking blood, a pipe set importantly between lips that relied on carrier pigeons to communicate. Confirmed bachelor, loving only his silk muse, named first Le Pôle Nord then promoted to stately Eagle. Pioneer explorer of the mammoth frozen wastes, homing in again and again, on the same ill-fated aim: flight. There are no blemishes, yet his sepia skin will ice-scorch, mottle, sickened by repeated bucolic feasts of polar bear steaks fried in their own rendered tallow. An atmosphere of hope and violence brews in camp, a white space pitched from driftwood and whalebone: snow-chinked walls, floor all floe (that will ultimately split and crash under the weight of dormant explorers). A burst of delirium, a sun dog's brilliant zeal, and it rises again from the balloon house, drifts ghost-slow, trailing its guide ropes like tail feathers and leaving a rift in the ice-capped sea. The shadow of the thing, yet not the thing itself – observed before lost; so, the past got all the flight.

II

Watch him stalk through studio dust, crouch low, then lower
still, to hatch a flickering full-throated firebird that twists and
dips in the glacial light, the flecked-metal air, a sudden twin-
shape sung from its shadows. Brancusi: fleeing a thousand
dusty miles from the Carpathian Mountains to Paris. His
pebble-wet eyes, a throb of folk tales in his blood, a cigar
tacked to lips relying on pidgin French to communicate.
Confirmed bachelor, loving his silvery mutt, Polaire,
named for the north star, plus a comely Parisian songstress.
Luminary explorer of modernism, repeating the same
migratory return to a tireless motif: flight. He buffed birds to
a shine from a patina like freckled skin to glossy forms that
would reflect his fêted bucolic feasts of forge-roasted chops,
haricots verts, drifts of snowy salt. An atmosphere of serenity
and tenderness in the white space made of arctic walls, of
skylights, of rubble and casts piled on floorboards (that would
bow and sink beneath the weight of their restless maestro).
A flash of recognition, then an iceblink in the flame, and the
bird reforms the abstract way: its hot bronze spirit distilled to
an experience of trilling, of wing-chirr, or a quill in a bottle
of gold ink. The essence of the thing, yet not the thing itself
– sensed sooner than seen; so, the mind gets all the flight.

Sleepless in Nyhavn – I

Your illness is that you're not able to cast a shadow.
—HANS CHRISTIAN ANDERSEN, 'The Shadow'

Begrudgingly, the landlady brings bread, coffee, a new candle.
Once she's rustled away (offering a small glance of pity),

he lights the new wick from the old yellow stump.
He holds the light close to the mirror to examine his lantern

face, and to try to see what other people see:
there, a line he didn't spot yesterday; here a new blemish;

and will you just look at that wild, untrimmed eyebrow!
His sigh extinguishes the candle. He lights it again,

and the room blooms, illuminated like the Tivoli at night,
its light picking out the glister of a spider camping out

on the window, its web pitched across filthy glass. He lifts
it off with a twist of paper ripped from a rejected manuscript,

then smiles when it drops into a dirty cup on the sill.
He watches it drown, silently willing his landlady to drink it.

PART TWO

either
A LITTLE BOY AND A LITTLE GIRL

or
HOME

But in childhood there is the tragedy of separation; there is, for instance, the typical event of being thrown out of Paradise, of having one's first shock of incompleteness and discovering that something perfect has been forever lost.

—MARIE-LOUISE VON FRANZ,
The Interpretation of Fairy Tales

Room

Woolf's great book about the room we need,
and the room we'll make with it.
            —ALI SMITH, *A Woolf of One's Own*

Deep winter, blue-black February, the hours
compacted in the flat all punctuated by the clunk
and groan of water slowing to glass
inside pipes that expand—expand—expand
            but never shatter.

There's a shortfall of blankets on the rental beds;
a meagre supply of heat (besides the teething
baby's cheeks, the toddler's fever dreams)
but we have gas for cooking and I'm glad for that.
            At least we still have gas.

The sitter quits, and again I am too bitter to fight,
so, sit glowering behind a frigid window,
watching frost thorns claw across car-hoods
as I trace the fug of my own condensed breath.
It liquifies and dribbles beyond a dark reflected desk
I cannot get to. I blow and I blow on fingers
too icy to type and feel nothing. I am nothing
but a mute landscape frantic for word-prints to happen.

You visit us unannounced,
the absent days unaccounted for,

all the gloam roses you can muster
—yet never an offer of childcare.

Instead, you forget your days,
let the phone bill go unpaid

as if your children's attachment
could ever be disconnected.

My God—
you wouldn't believe the gyre of violence

in my mind when you sneer
at my little scribbled fictions, written

in the snotty pockets of naptimes.
Could you do this? Live

in a menagerie of shitty feelings:
primal—messy—formless

clambering self over self over fractious self,
some triumvirate of murderous rage.

In this place, every little death
(natural/unnatural)
is jarred and stored; exhibited,
and what's generative is left to rot
because alone I cannot preserve it.

Listen—
I don't want to be admired,
denied, or fetishised to justify
my life or vindicate my human rights.
I don't have to accept your bizarre
projections or risk your wrath,
you bastard, I'm through with that.

What I need is freedom to roam
this various and complicated mind,
and room—a room I can call my own.
A quiet room. A heated room.
Preferably with a lock on the door.

Feast Days

Easter in Finland, and the children
dress up as little witches: old aprons, borrowed shawls,
baskets slung from arm-crooks while sticky fingers
grip willow switches glittered and stuck with feathers.
I'm thinking of you and your sweet tooth as I sit at this iced
Helsinki window watching them perform
a door-to-door sorcery, cackling and dancing for treats.

Darling—
let's conjure a north westerly powerful enough
to whip us away from here; spin us
up the Gulf of Bothnia to that coastline littered with islets.
Let's stake a claim—you and I—build a cabin
like Tove and Tuulikki's. We'll settle beside an inlet
with a lopsided deck, fish for dinner from an old red rowboat,
and swim wearing nothing but flower-crowns.

Afterward, we'll huddle over mugs in the dark,
comb each other's hair, and flick through old recipe books.
I'll lead you over to the stove to show you
how to make *mämmi*: that oozy, gooey, finicky dessert
that children never like. We'll need handfuls of malt, of rye,
jugs of warm water, sugar, and a long coil of orange zest.
We'll take days and days to fold—prove—fold,
and we'll stretch out time while watching those soft bubbles
rise and rise until we're beside ourselves with wanting,
not yet believing there'll be time enough to feast.

Watching *Frozen* with the Kids

2014

When you're small, it's not hard to be enchanted
by the way you kneel before the TV: eyes wide, mouths slung
open, snacks suspended in mid-air
as you take in the untrue beauty of digital princess sisters.
I want to educate you on the realities of Lapland in winter,
the indigenous people who live there, and how climate
catastrophes are make herding harder each season.
I want to tell you it's unrealistic that Ana doesn't freeze
to death, and that the bridge she sings from breaks
every law of physics. But I let it go, find myself unable
(and unwilling, yet) to dismantle your winter wonderland.

2022

February half term and I'm lying on the sofa reading
Joelle's C+nto. My teens are bored, both wanting
to re-watch *Frozen*, but not to admit it. *Do you want to build
a snowman?* Oh, shut up, bitch. Hey! What?
Sorry for being insensitive, but your parents are about to die.
My son used to love Olaf the snowman, so I glance
up to watch him revisit this scene. *So, this is heat? I love it!*
You literally melt, honey-booboo, my daughter mocks,
and something is suddenly lost for my son. I just remembered
how scary this movie is, he says. That man looks like Putin,
points out his sister. He's a bit of a c+nto, isn't he?

Midnight Trees

I watch you kick off your pumps,
peer inside the havoc of your room
and watch you guzzle a blue glass
of milk so urgently, noisily, it dribbles
down your neck: makes you shudder.

Later, in the garden, we dress
our midnight trees until snowfall
makes dust of our chattering.
You blink twice, link my arm
and whisper 'Sauna, Mama?' I nod.

You sprawl along the wooden ledge
beside me: all barely there breasts,
a new dark between your legs,
each pale limb lengthening, sapling-
strong, to ladder the slatted walls.

Your hot upturned face almost smiles
as I lift a ribbon of your damp hair
stuck to my thigh. Treasured girl; firstborn
child, how I relish that light in your eyes,
before the steam-veil falls between us.

Citadel of Salt

A gallon of tears can yield three ounces of salt;
salt enough to preserve an unclear memory.

It would be two lifetimes before I understood it:
that feeling behind the lighthouse beyond Løkken.

.We fell apart, spun out fast, wheeling from cliff-edge
hands free, shoulders and hips angling into bends

and throwing our devotions to the open-faced sun.
We stopped damp, panting, hiked the dunes,

our legs getting scritch-scratched for just an hour's
bob and list in the tea-green sea. Afterward,

you pawed wet sand up against me, slapped at it
to immure me in a citadel of salt: fortified with pebble

walls, a razor clam drawbridge knit shut with weed,
a ragged gull feather stuck in its crumbling turret.

How the heat swelled and prickled my skin, a kiln
domed over my pinned limbs making a tender-fleshed

fish of me baked under a crust (flake by sweet white
flake), or a lost child buried under two-day snow.

Come Home
after Tua Forsström

Come home from the city gates.
Come home from the river's wintry lid.
Like a child with scuffed cheeks,
ice skates slung over your blades,
come home. A riddle
reigns, your absence puzzles,
days all feel the same:
bottles on a freezing sill brim-full of menses,
tears. It's a question of not forgetting.
It's a question of not forgetting that night
in fur on the great white sleigh, real
as any dreaming!
Once upon a time we were attic to attic.
Once upon a time there were roses, rose petals
until one of us had to vanish,
our moment left prone, prone but unopened.
I teach children to tie their little sleds
to the back of a farmer's cart
but all the while I'm holding out
for your iced face in the crowd, come home.

Sleepless in Nyhavn – II

Lad mig ved dit Hjerte slumre ind.
 —HANS CHRISTIAN ANDERSEN, 'De Døende Barn'

Sunday, and all night the stories wouldn't come.
He was trying to write about a siren, a nymph, a nereid
who lured sailors to their watery deaths.
He rises edgy from his desk, distracted by noises
seeping beneath salt-sealed windows.
He pushes them apart, leans out to the sound of gulls
screaming, foghorns blowing, rigging hitting masts—
everything beyond him damp and pulsing and lapping.
Nyhavn has its own particular stink:
sailors and the fishing boats they spill from,
rust-coloured spume dribbling from their portholes;
sewage running along the cobbles to empty into the canal;
cheap perfume rising from those strange acts
that take place in alleys, doorways, under a ship's ballast.
A fishwife with a foul mouth and bloodied apron
reminds him of his mother, she who muffled
the guttural sounds of pleasure while her giant child
hid his shaking face under a pillow, feigning sleep
across the foot of the overshared marital bed.
And even though she was no good, he liked her familiar
smell of soap, of lye, and gin when she could afford it.

PART THREE

either
AN ENCHANTED FLOWER GARDEN

or
RIVER

Many fairy-tale heroes, at a crucial point in their development, fall into a deep sleep or are reborn. Each reawakening or rebirth symbolizes the reaching of a higher stage of maturity and understanding.

—BRUNO BETTELHEIM, *The Uses of Enchantment*

The Sorrows of Young Gerda

after 'Disappointed Love', (1821) by Francis Danby

~~Grandmother,~~ Dearest Grandmother,

I'm sorry for your loss. I'm sorry for the wasted inheritance;
I'm sorry for the cost of having to comb and drag this ~~shitty~~
river. My locket's under the linden tree, my stockings,
pocketbook, purse ~~(for what it's worth)~~. I know this is no
way to repay you—I who have wanted for nothing, yet still
want almost everything I cannot have (and so fiercely). ~~And
didn't you warn me he'd leave me for that wintry bitch?! I can
hear your *tsk*; the in-suck of breath through your puckered
lips—the ones that never kiss.~~ I have all this having, yet after
him there's not a thing I can cling to. I am all longing: longing
to make you proud, to feel lit up, to jettison these quirks and
deficits ~~instead of aching for his hard freckled arms around
my waist; the taste of his lemony skin.~~ Oh, Grandmother,
you taught me how to change minds, tyres, bandages, but
I have no clue how to weather this storm, this stress; this
devastation of not being necessary. ~~But how could you ever
fathom lust or sorrow? You with your dungarees, whiskered
chin, self-sufficient ways. You who need no body, no human
touch. How could you ever know how much it mattered that I
needed to call myself somebody's… anybody's?~~

~~Yours,~~ Gerda

P. S. I've ruined my new red shoes.

River Red Shoes

Hot unhappy girls,
how much you give away,
                    your most treasured, buried possessions:
            all that lust, that spite, that rage.
                            Do not follow Ophelia,
                split off from her vital self,
        one part floating floral,
                    her others rambling, wild.

            Girls,
        I've had my fill of it:
                how you come thrusting at me
with your letters, petals, stones,
            come begging me to return
                    you to yourselves or grant wishes
        to live solely in the reflected places
(as though I could blot out all body, all hurt).

            Sweet Gerda,
        you choke me at my source.
                    Little-knowing how much I want you
        to thrive in your new red shoes,
to follow them where they must go,
            for they know, surely, they know.

Waterbodies

water water almost clear
we can make our activity not contribute
to pollution do no harm to the fabric of
our region as
we wholeheartedly
commit to zero pollutions
we must rise overnight we
must cha nge Direction o n
climate incidents. Our country,
ever passing through extremes can
cause huge volumes of excess
to enter our systems, while
waterbodies become more sensitive The landscape
—low-lying, with slow-flowing rivers,
can be challenge d our people,
tackling it at root cause give us tools
to measure and track progress We are
committed to
carrying water in a spirit
of transparency to protect our current
and future joy

Washerwoman & Son

Washday in Odense, and Hans straggles behind a mother
who stops not briefly for gossip over the asylum wall

before heading off to the river to scrub other people's smalls.
She clip-clop waddles through town, across the fields,

her chilblained feet in straw-stuffed clogs, sleeves rolled up
over plump elbows, her dried hands rubbed in pig fat.

Gangly Hans—all arms and legs—struggles to hold on
to the theatre of his own desires (keeps a puppet in his pocket

made from a peg dressed in snippets of shoe leather). He
drifts behind his mother, dreamy for applause, fame, the feel

of red velvet against his cheek. She grabs his wrist to hurry
him along, her calloused hands making contact scratch.

He squirms free and vanishes into the gleaning fields,
a separation that renders both mother and son relieved.

She gets down to work, breasts wobbling as she paddles
at other people's stains, beats at her own reflection to displace

all her faces in the water. She doesn't notice her flaxen-
haired son peeking from the reeds, or how he takes note

of her three acts of rage: the scrubbing, the dunking,
the thwacking of sheets against rocks, their patchworked

centres worn thin as breath-holes on frosted glass.
All the while, Hans picks wildflowers, writes up his dramas

in his mind, sings to self-soothe. When his mother glances
up from suds and looks along the riverbank at other women,

their part-hidden grins, she throws a glare over her shoulder
at her soft-voiced boy—her ugly duckling son—to arrest

his high-pitched singing. He catches the shame or rage
coming off her, but turns away from it to transmute

it into pride, crowning himself with a garland of flowering
weeds as he forages in the understory for more tales.

Something Rotten

after 'Black Apples', (1999) by Kiki Smith

> Women clasp their daughters to their breasts and whisper
> horrors into their ears: Darkness. Appetites. Trees.
> —SARAH SHUN-LIEN BYNUM, *Madeleine is Sleeping*

She is woken by woodcutters, the buzz of them, the hum of sweat as they hack
rot from heartwood after the apples came in like blackened breasts.

Unbinding herself from sleep—from dust-weighted sheets—she observes these men
damp at their dirty work and feels little but listless where she used to be restless,

back when her sap was still able to rise. Under some sad spell she'd fallen
to a hundred-year sleep, this whey-faced girl who dreamt a labyrinth of mirrors,

this abandoned child who knew not which route to choose; was unable to guess
which reflected self might be true. Raised on gossip and missives and gimcrack wisdom

by old maids peddling a performance of womanhood, their faces painted over dusted,
ruddy gooseflesh, their heartbreaks all stored in the same worm-eaten place;

these undated ladies in their circuses of hurt, dead set on spinning fiction from unruly truth.
They sniffed out desire before she could nurse or murder it, cautioned her (spital-firing)

that the only place for a tongue was bitten between her teeth, as though children were unwise
or as slack-jawed as their adults. There was something wild-to-excited in their pious, unlooking glass

eyes, the way they raised blades to the very thought of her carnalities, forced her to decompose love
letters she never wrote, or face expulsion from the garden where she'd come to dread her own

budding, for fear of drowning in a fug of blowsy flowers. Those shattering operatics
she's so keen to leave behind, urged on by something real, something only sensed at the edge

of memory: that lifeblood throb of full body longings for girls, and only girls, who in their very
essence offer a deeper, darker, softer erotic joy. There—oh there—lies her happy ever after.

Starflowers

She fills the soil with chamomile and marigold, with hyssop and sage,
borage and angelica, with wormwort and feveriew. She installs
seven skeps at the furthest edge of the garden; on warm July days it
is possible to hear the restless rumble of the bees from the house.
—MAGGIE O'FARRELL, *Hamnet*

At the tail-end of spring, I'll come to understand
why I tucked a last-minute packet of starflower
seeds in with your Christmas gift (a marker for the book),
their deep blue beauty a beacon for the bees.
I understand it when I cry watching *Ammonite*,
the scene where Mary lets herself into Mrs Philpot's garden
and she glances up, delighted. I know it then,
that all I want is for a woman to turn to me like that,
a radiant warmth in her eyes, for her to smile saying my name
in that soft, familiar way that lets me know I am welcome.

My internet search tells me that starflowers are borage,
borage meaning courage. Perhaps I hoped you'd do the dirty
work of growing, and by proxy constellate a fearlessness
in me. Now I accept that only I can do it: journey
through my own black earth's network of tangled roots
to fix the original trip switch and connect myself up
to a full circuit of feelings: the low steady thrum of them—a
hive of sweet activity somewhere out of sight—that lets
a newly ignited heat rush uninterrupted to my filaments, flush
my system with a liquid gold that lights me from the inside.

Daisy | Daisy

after Ophelia (2018) & Star Wars: The Last Jedi (2017)

A long time ago in a galaxy far, far away a princess died & lived on in her followers while a flyby falcon circled a dirty scavenger girl dancing a barefoot devotional before a traitor queen: her fickle majesty sipping from a bird skull, coiled inside it a heart-stopping toxin.

Midnight on the ramparts, all of Denmark sleeping dreamless, uneasy. All but the gravedigger fool skulking in the shadows, a bloom of night-weed in his cap, his hot blood thumping & his howls disembodied as he watches a prince & his own dark twin duel at the brink between worlds, their white-hot sabre sparks igniting the night sky & making constructs burn.

Sunrise in a bad place from an old war. In the blue-grey smoke of dawn a ray of hope rises from the dark side—still hidden in unknown regions—& casts a spectral light through the salt spray on the bridge of a listing ship, right where a son rants: *You're just a memory!* somewhere close to his father's ghost.

Alone in the forest, no girl sings of a fallow heart in the language of flowers, no girl floats in a river's murk or sinks to some underground terrain. Instead, she levitates cross-legged, no longer able to clone her emotions or apprentice herself to the whims of others. She channels a feeling, a force beyond rage, just this signal emitting: Be with me.

The symbol sent is a dagger cut with glyphs, an Inuit wayfinder, a map, a prism of green crystal glowing to show her how to unfollow the co-ordinates of her ancestors. She claims this strange augury—its lightspeed way of releasing memory from object—tucks it into her boot & begins her quest.

In this system, where the dead speak back in mysterious broadcasts, a woman's voice is the only one she's ever trusted, the only clear voice she's even heard through these revisionist histories that echo with the same old wars & dead kings. It's a woman's voice that returns—not to haunt, but to remind— the time has come: her weakness is her strength, she has everything she needs, & she must go on alone, even with fear & trembling.

She takes a first step—unsteady—two sides struggling to guard her unmastered heart: I'm ready; I'm not ready. She knows she is pawn & receptacle for men's deceptions. She knows she is a fighter-pilot & curse breaker of her generation. She knows, too—beyond all other knowing—that even unmothered & severed from that initial, primitive source: she is also all the Jedi.

PART FOUR

either

THE PRINCE AND THE PRINCESS

or

KINGDOM

By making children the heroes and heroines of such fairy tales, the erotic discoveries and ordeals many of them describe had to be disinfected—leaving sexuality latent in violent symbols and gory plots.

—MARINA WARNER, *Six Myths of Our Time*

A Forest Opera

I returned to the woods of childhood, afraid of the dark
green silence but wanting to be alone, wanting also
that sense of a trusted other close by. Beyond the river,
beyond the trees, I thought I saw the hint of a figure
on the path, but as I walked under the canopy of cool leaves,
it transformed before me into silver birch, leaning
in the breeze, soft and calm in her mossy velvet dress,
her taffeta shadows. I felt my heart arrive and knew I was safe.
I touched her trunk—her rough bark and wrinkled skin—
pressed my cheek to it and whispered my fears.
She scooped me up in her branches and held me close,
(so close I could hear the sap rising inside her). Time slowed,
and beneath the sounds of my breathing—my heart
an off-beat metronome—beneath the birdsong and sunshine,
low, low notes like fine roots began to surface
from the undergrowth. I heard small furry beings rustle
undercover; a dog chasing scents through the nettles
and splashing into the dyke where spores and willow-seed
floated over the water. Nearby, a soft whirr as mayflies
yo-yoed the air. As this sound-world bound itself
around me—trumpet flowers like open mouths—all
the voices of the forest congregated into one glorious chorus:
an evergreen crescendo, dismantling the soaked-up quiet.

Ravenish

But it is so difficult to speak your language!
Do you understand Ravenish? If so, I can tell you much better.
                    —HANS CHRISTIAN ANDERSEN, *The Snow Queen*

She talked back, but he didn't understand
her raven language of harsh caws and soft croaks.
                    —AUDREY NIFFENEGGER, *Raven Girl*

After the garden—that long unpollinated sleep—
it is suddenly not summer. Mist rises off the river,
brittle leaves curl and fall, and I am lost here in bitter
autumn; lost in thorny raven country. Sitting on a boulder
to rub my bluing feet, I come to feel observed by a presence
in a pine tree, and I wish it was an emissary to guide me.
In a flash of silver-black, the huge crack of a wingspan,
he drops—all strut and flutter—and hops
around me like a boxer, this one-eyed scruff of a bird:
whiskers around his beak, a ruff of dysregulated feathers,
hinged wings, purple-green in this half-light,
his head at a quizzical tilt. He edges close—enticed
by anything that winks treasure—and eyes the last sloe
from my pocket, leaves a solitary pinfeather in payment,
rasps as he eats it, then lets out a *kek*, a *quork*, a cantankerous
caw I cannot fathom. I want it to mean: *Keep going,
keep going, don't turn back.* I want him to be saying: *Yes,
I've seen something brotherish in the shadowy palace where my
tame beloved roosts. Follow me, Gerda, I'll take you there.*

Goldings

Winter nineteen-ninety-nine in small-town Suffolk
and I accompany you to the posh shop
to help you choose a waistcoat for my wedding.

We stop first at The Star for squid, Abbot Ale,
and another chance for you to beat me at bar billiards.
In Goldings, I follow you past the shelves of red

or yellow chinos, endless checky shirts, so many Barbours
I'm almost entirely disenchanted. You call me
into the changing room for my opinion, I murmur

you look perfect in the pale gold printed with *fleur de lys*.
I stand behind as you look at yourself in the mirror,
kiss your cheek and take a mental picture I'm glad for now.

Paying at the till, you take a bobble hat from a rack
and pull it over my face, laughing: *that's better!*
followed by something muffled, potentially affectionate,

that got lost in the static of my hair. It's moth-eaten now,
the bobble long lost to a cat, but I still wear
it for winter river swims, or simply when I miss you.

Fool's Gold

after 'Crowning' (2013), by Tom de Freston

All hail and grime and flecks and spores
smeared by mucky fingers, sucked and dipped in pollen,
sulphide, the gold pots.

Everything wanes without her:
the folds of my belly, the tufts of my pits,
these thumbed-in eye sockets, and a lupus itching my pod
like the mottle on a looking glass no vinegar can touch.

Feel it like a man, they say, *dispute it like a man.*
Yet I'm wedded only to impotence,
shrunk to the nothing of a blind writhing bairn
frantic to scratch at the lustrous face
of its distant/present mother—yes,
the full-milked white of her: she who raises tides
and men to her puppetry of lips and nipples and gorging.

O gentle lady, why must I keep alone? Hide my fires,
extinguish such desires, banish this pair of wrestling fools
hell bent on their primal scene.

I've become strange, a stranger to myself,
cast out in gilt, and furs, smoked mirrors; unable to see
what's treasured besides a crown now barbed and hollow.

I keep my shadow tethered to a chair leg,
have no agency with the need to rule all I crave or run from,
spend small, tortured hours (little murdered sleeps)
dreaming then dreading
moments given over to delight, to destruction.

Come you spirits of the fetid air,
come you three of poisoned cups, I conjure you
maidens of mirth and vituperative deeds
to spit on this king and make him shine—please?

Dancing Queen

Let no one invite me, for I will not dance.
———SØREN KIERKEGAARD, *Philosophical Fragments*

Dance she did, and dance she must, straight out into the dark wood.
———HANS CHRISTIAN ANDERSEN, 'The Red Shoes'

We are late to the *Snow Widows* talk, late
from lunch and another bite at our ongoing
conversation about whether I am chorophobic.
You ask me again—you, with your dream
of a silent disco barefoot in a meadow—how it feels
to be so afraid of dancing, I tremble at weddings,
used to hide out in nightclub toilets
soft rocking and finger-blocking my ears.
I want to tell you that it's not a lack of desire
to let go, and I don't think I am unwilling to
relinquish myself to a pulse that isn't my own, no.

Still trying to carve out what it is from what it isn't,
the speaker describes Kathleen Scott as 'mad
for dancing' on a visit to New York in 1913.
You nudge me and grin, let your granny specs slip
to the end of your nose to make me laugh.

I like it when you do that. And I like the way
you rest an arm along the back of my chair
when you sense I'm anxious. And—even though
it makes me blanch—I kind-of-like the times
you try to entice me to explore your joy of dance.

We hug and we hug by the iced-up gates
to the Botanics, you tap my frown line and say:
We've got to get you out of your mind
and into your body. Later—craving warmth—
I revisit this shivering on a frost-furred bench,
fingers so cold I can hardly hold open my notebook,
limbs twitching; making jerky, unruly movements.
Uneasy, I stamp my feet, then stop to breathe
in the buds of a cherry tree, its almost-blossom
just promising something new. And I write:
If I danced with anyone, it would be with you.

Undiscovered Country

I wake from her kiss, the pulsing dream of it,
want only for her to cup my face and lift me—dripping—to her lips.
Requited love, I know no touch of it.
I have longed long, even while her smiling told me no.
And I have cried to hear, just once: *the queen desires you.*
She stroked my hair, and that was love begun,
some part of me feeding on its wonder, like a guilty
creature in the forest by the brook.
Deep inside my closet a kind of fighting kept me from sleep,
nights hideous until I conjured her, good Gertrude—*let this be so*—
spent all on dread pleasures sprung from neglected touch.
I'd toss and turn, and pray and burn: *stay illusion!*
Or, *let it be tenable.* Let the door be locked no longer on desire.
Let us speak not in words, but a wondrous double
tonguing—hot, soft, slow—where I'd tremble, look pale,
unfold myself as though my flesh would melt in defeated joy.
My pearl is hers and there's the rub:
this little organ lightly touched offers up its thousand
natural shocks (only!) to the queen of buried Denmark.
She tells me I am welcome in Elsinore, but I have stayed too long
seeing unseen: eyes without feeling, feeling without sight.
If she'd look twice, she'd find me capable of my own distress,
no ghosted or cracked Ophelia clinging
to a snatched-back happiness where, often, madness hits.
I will not regret the many tenders wrung from me—green girl,
fool of nature—my heart unfortified, no watchman on it.
I own them, alone, set naked on her kingdom—in frailty, yes—
but with this dizzying freedom to be, or not be. Either go no further
across this distracted globe. Or go softly on, broken open by knowing
her body must remain to me an undiscovered country.

Quicksilver

Christ, I am that woman who finds a pickled herring
so devastating she may never recover.
I am her: she who tastes a soft beauty in fish
and must write about its sweet, nipple-pink flesh;
who licks the silvered skin (then sucks on her own fingers!)
for a last salt-edged kick, and—O—that sublime tang.

PART FIVE

either
THE LITTLE ROBBER MAIDEN

or
FOREST

Afeared or not, it is an act of deepest love to allow oneself to be stirred by the wildish soul of another.

—CLARISSA PINKOLA ESTES,
Women Who Run with the Wolves

Sleepless in Nyhavn - III

... let me have true evidence of your respect—if and when I deserve
it—then—oh! please do not be angry with me—say 'Du' to me!
—HANS CHRISTIAN ANDERSEN,
Letter to Edvard Collin, 19th May 1831

I lie here thinking of you—burning—dear Edvard,
my almost-brother, my would-be lover, master-

servant if that's what you'd like. So many nights
I wish you'd come to me in these still, small hours

and let me show you the ways you are adored.
Don't be repulsed, all I want is human kindness:

your breath—your heft—a handful of salt.
Perhaps I'll be ashamed of this come morning,

afraid of my own brief courage. But for now,
let me be bold (if undeserving), bold and honest

enough to request we lessen the distance between us.
You have no idea how my heart is beating as I write,

how I could never ask this while meeting your eyes,
but if you think of me too, say Du to me, say Du.

No Bones

You came and I was longing for you.
You cooled a heart that burned with desire.
                    —ANNE CARSON, *If Not, Winter: Fragments of Sappho*

The girl with the beautiful beard—almost blue
in the moonlight—eyes me over the fire while she eats.
Her unbroken stare, a half-smile on those greasy lips
(I want to lick) leaves no room for ambiguity.

If I wasn't sitting on this stump, I'd lose my legs
from under me, my spine a python writhing in desire.
I watch her spit her scraps into the ashes, stretch
back and make a tremendous, animal moan.
She holds her plait behind her neck, leans forward,
and uses a white-hot ember to light her pipe.

I can't not watch her suck on it. She stands
so abruptly, I panic. She swears at her fellow bandits;
punches the odd arm, then cracks her knuckles one-by-one
and leaves. A few paces into the trees, she glances
over her shoulder and beckons for me to follow.

My God, you don't even want to know how fast I dash
after her, my vulva pulses: flame-lit, flickering

Robbergirls

You were the prettiest little trinket
these sooted eyes had ever seen,
& yet I robbed you of your defences:
laid you out on a bed of straw, slipped you
dripping from your hood, your furs,
those damn rabbitskin boots.
You wept when I licked the iced glister
from your breasts; dust-kissed your ribs;
spread heat & delight between your thighs.
We wintered on whispers & firelight,
& my hundred smoky turtledoves peeping
from the rafters seemed like poets, rolling love
on their tongues instead of ashes.

Slipping from her mother's whiskered skins,
she haunts my tangled forest dreams,
a bandit in snicking thickets. She creeps
under cover of leafmould, fingerblades grazing
my lips, strips me of my mantle, my kirtle,
those damn rabbitskin boots.
Pinned between her jack-knifed limbs, a scent
of flame & fury rises from her skin;
a flapping rabble of filthy mockingbirds
laughing from the rafters. Backbone to whetted
backbone, I steal from her choking stranglehold,
drag her kicking heart from its unlocked chest,
spit on the embers of her desire, & flee.

Pikku Valkko

In the listening forest,
a smear on the edge of vision,
a shift away from solitude
and I sense you:
pikku valkko, little white,
almost hidden but for a young rack
of frosty antlers, the smallest pink
of your damp muzzle,
a touch of red daubed about your eyes.
Snowy calf, when you stop,
glance back—witness me teetering
on the sill between the here
and the not-here,
your look is almost wounded.
Yet, still, you vanish into silvered trees
leaving me free to stumble in,
stumble out of a shivering wisdom.
Fleeting beauty, celestial bull,
I still hear the music of your bell.

* pikku valkko – Finnish for 'little white reindeer'

Stole

_____This poem doesn't have a first line
because another poem stole it. Gerda—bloodthirsty
little monster, perfect weasel in her white
stage—filched what I was loath to give, snatched it as I slept,
pillaged from my chest, and lifted my hush-hush secret.
It was mine to tell of slipping from my mother's
whiskered skins, tiptoeing the bitten forest to curl smoke-like
around a girl—a feckless girl—who flirted with
the peril of loving me. And I don't even care
that she purloined two hares from my roasting spit,
a fist of bitter berries, some blackened bread. But she fled
on my stupidest reindeer, harnessed its tenderised heart,
fed it on promises, promises, itty-bitty kisses,
the false salt of her doe-eyed tears.
My untamed dreams steal back to her at night.
Awakening violence, I rise to whet my flensing knives,
imagine her silenced, snow-frozen, toes black as the tips
of ermine tails. Ermine: the pest that would rather surrender
to death than have me spoil her pristine pelt.
I'll hunt her down, follow the urge for her destruction
that's become a kind of lust in me. I will crisscross her path
with jagged trap lines, drag my kill to the deepest dark; sniff it,
paw it, tear it apart, and uncover its intricate workings.

The Ermine Myth

I stole her heart away and put ice in its place.
—CHARLES DICKENS, *Great Expectations*

Summer solstice and a snowstorm of moths smothers
the bird cherry trees on Jesus Green, turning them to a plague
of fine ladies muting their sticky-beaked chatter.
They are stripped clean of their leaves, each one draped
in a veil of singed webs—of burn-blistered skin—they lean
in posing as an avenue of ghosts. I eye them, blind
to the shuttered house of my own dark stasis, this unrequited
desire that fires on stories I tell myself about loving, and
of being loved. *That's one way to have your cake and not eat it*,
my therapist says. I watch shrieking kids poke at the gore,
then peel the flaking limbs until each debrided wound
is returned to the first stage of healing: a misery of virginal
decay. I think of Miss Havisham's mottled stockings,
that long life away from sunlight, and my own conviction
that I bind myself to a similar kind of widowhood.
The moths are stunning, hung like felted decorations,
but they're eating the trees alive. It's hard to believe
they won't die, that they'll survive, and only be weakened
for a season. Even when the sun is highest in the sky,
they look as though they've remained in winter under
the darkest star—Estella—a marsh king's daughter: cruel, cold,
unobtainable to what tries to germinate and live long in Pip.

The Suspended Forest

Silkscreen trees, like an audience walk-through to a theatre,
a fairy tale: strange and magical, beautiful
and dangerous, peopled by spirits, tree folk, guardians:
those whose simple joy it is to green our world,
to strengthen our roots and nourish the rich inner
landscape. Pick any tree to stand beneath in the bluebells
and the wild garlic, then listen—

                                        birds nesting, wildlife
emerging; sounds of rustling and creaking, the smell of moss
and earth and rotting leaves. This is our ecosystem,
this forest design, defined by nature, networked, regenerative
and embedded with a timescale larger than our own:
the long life of the tree and this fleeting human moment.
To this circle, you are called to give thanks for the tree
nursery that secretly sips the soil: each filigree branch,
each buttery leaf, each winged seed key that now has space
to move, stretch, breathe, and grow into huge elm, venerable
oak, anchored in strength and integrity. Old whisperer,
silhouetted against the sky in winter: you big, kissable,
dependable giant. From ground to crown in all your resilience
and hope, all your asymmetry and imperfection,
we have gathered in this small patch of tranquillity to say
you are magnificent; you keep us grounded; you are perfect
as all trees are; we stand stronger under cover of your canopy.
        We are blessed to have inherited the tree.

PART SIX

either
THE LAPLAND WOMAN AND
THE FINLAND WOMAN

or
FIRE

She is her own woman, a parthogenetic mother, and she decides on a case-by-case basis whether she will help or kill the people who come to her hut.

—JACK ZIPES, *The Irresistible Fairy Tale*

Homelands

High on the fells and hidden,
I sit amongst saxifrage,
lichen, and dwarf-birches on the turn;

sit squinting over tops
of tiny, pointed firs
five times as high as any library stacks;

sit in awe of these rust-coloured slopes,
these unnavigable blue-black
lakes as I lean back against a god-like stone,

close my eyes and absently pluck plump
bilberries from a bush beside me,
burst them in my mouth, purpling my tongue.

It is in this idle moment, I slowly come to know
(know also that it cannot be true):
that Lapland, for me, tastes like home.

Lapland Summer

a translation of 'Lapin Kesä', (1902) by Eino Leino

In Lapland, plant-life thrives so briefly:
the grass, the barley, even the dwarf birch trees.
It's something I reflect on deeply
when I think of my people who lived here before me.

Why does everything beautiful have to die,
all that's hardy wilt and rot away?
Why do so many of us fear we'll lose our minds?
Why so few can be soothed by the *kantele*?

Up here, even the sturdiest tend to perish
cut down whilst in their prime.
Those with desires, hopes, and families they cherish
scythed like hay long before their time.

Elsewhere, I've heard of silver-haired elders
who live long, still with fire in their eyes.
So why do the youth here seem lost and bewildered,
encountering death with little surprise?

I don't even know why I dwell on such things,
is it my own mind's disintegration?
I wish I felt as inspired to realise my own dreams,
instead of sighing at the state of my nation.

Maybe I could blame the short-lived Lapland sun,
for these grief-filled, long, lonely hours
that have me pine for birdsong, for light, and for fun
that last longer than our fleet summer flowers.

But winter's grip feels like one endless night
that freezes my thoughts to nothing but icy wastes,
and all of my best ideas take flight
like birds of passage departing this frigid place.

Oh, white birds, Lapland's summer guests,
when you vanish you dash our hopes.
Won't you consider overwintering here,
build your nests on our coasts, fells, and slopes?

I wish you would delay your southward journey
and teach us (how much we could learn!)
to trust in our minds' innate migratory urges;
and have faith that spring will return.

I mourn you as you fly away from me,
swoop, dive, and glide across the world's snowy dome.
The moment you hear we are again winter-free,
oh, bold ideals, I beg you, please, come home.

kantele – a musical instrument from Finnish myth

Curled Up in Her Language Nest

The culture is alive only when the language is alive.
—Marja-Liisa Olthuis, Suvi Kivelä, and Tove Skutnabb-Kangas,
Revitalising Indigenous Languages: How to Recreate a Lost Generation

Late May in Sápmi and there's a drip-drip of snowmelt, a sky full of birds returning, and deep in the forest, spindly-legged reindeer calves come bleating into being. I log on for my first Northern Sámi class, and my teacher—Suvi—speaks fast. *Pyeri!* I blink. *Hello!* She beams at me from her remote language nest, and her voice is a voice to curl up to. She takes me through the alphabet—all thirty-two letters—and by the end of the lesson I can sound out my name: *kuo-bâr, aa-bis, päd-di, päd-di, lye-mi.* By June, I open with an uncertain *Tiervâ.* Suvi grins and returns my greeting. *Kii tun la?* Who are you? Good question, I think, as I begin to formulate an answer. *Mun lam Kaddy.* She nods. *Kii Kaddyid?* Which Kaddy are you, what is your parentage? *Mun lam Paul Benyon Kaddy,* I reply. I ache at saying your name. July comes with the midnight sun. Suvi roams me on her smartphone past a woodshed, a splintering sled, a silvering old smoke sauna at the lake's edge, *jävri.* She touches a rowboat, *käärbis,* lifts a net, *viermi,* shakes her head at finding her husband's unsheathed hunting knife, *nijbe,* abandoned on the seat. Early autumn—blueberries carpeting her garden—Suvi has advanced me to more complex constructions, but I stumble on a particular phrase: *Mun ahevušám tuu.* I long for you. You see, it doesn't just translate Gerda to the Robbergirl, but also—Dad—me to you.

Only Hope

A poet goes herding in northern Finland and finds herself
not in a forest but the sealed beige Soviet-looking headquarters
of the Reindeer Herders' Association. Her guide
has laid out all the kit she'll need: cable knit socks,
moon boots (huge), mitts thick as oven gloves, a neon vest.

She walks awkward as an astronaut to the parking lot,
folds her entire wadded body into a car that will speed her north
on studded tyres. Veering between mines and wind turbines,
over pipelines and under power lines that crisscross the tundra,
she hears about a cousin lost to a river: his snowmobile sunk
under sun-weakened ice. It isn't even melt-season,
but there's a too-wet blizzard puttering the glass, some still-green
trees leaning in like drunks, the ground beneath them soupy, boggy.
Those that have uprooted leave craters like open wounds,
ice-veins thawing and peat-rich soil defrosting to release a toxic
brew of more methane and carbon than the atmosphere
can metabolise. She opens the window to peer out,
and there's a stink of decay from organic matter resurfacing
from permafrost: mammoth tusks pushing up like gruesome buds.

Deep inside the forest, she hears them before she sees them:
the way they half-snort, half-honk, as they snaffle at bark
crocheted with the grey-green lichen they like to eat;
the wood-on-wood locking of antlers still hung with autumn's
velvet rags; and that snapping—not of campfire—but the tiny bones
in their ankles that skittishly click to warn of nearby threats.
There are predators, yes: bear, and lynx, and wolverine.
But industry too with its thirst for fossil fuels,
and the constant scouring for new deposits: extraction activities

unsettling the ground and trampling healthy pasturage.
This is a world on the edge of panic: birds out of season,
families displaced, hungry wolves wondering too close to towns.
You can see it in the eyes of the buff-coloured reindeer cows:
heckles raised by the urgent chime of iced branches
just before they rear up to fight capture, detach from their young
kicking—bucking—grunting when caught by lasso-throwing herders.

The polar vortex is like a lasso. In full health, it's meant to harness
and contain the bitter-cold jet stream that spins above the North Pole.
But when it weakens, goes slack, Arctic blasts can drift too far
south and trigger other weather anomalies: forest fires, landslides,
floods: those life-or-death warnings of a cycle out of synch.

Here in the forest, the air is thick with sweat, with sap, dusts of ice.
Herding work is year-round hard: any gains lost instantly
to the cost of machinery, fuel, supplemental feed.
Herders rely on the polar environment for their livelihoods,
survival, yet their cryosphere is close to collapse. Too late,
we have realised that the treasures of the north must stay frozen,
snowed over, locked up in Artic soil and ice. This region
is warming twice as fast as elsewhere, faster than the planet can adapt.
We cannot repair the damage. Our only hope is to slow things.

Grace Notes

If you forgive, he would say, you may indeed still not understand,
but you will be ready to understand, and that is the posture of grace.
                                        —MARILYNNE ROBINSON, *Home*

Day 4: New snow, a weight on my chest, in my bones,
the creak of my boots as I trek the frozen *Palojärvi*, aching.
An hour from camp, I am ice-crusted, damp; crest-fallen.
The herders warned wolves, lynx, and even bear wander here,

but I do not care, cannot fear in this white silence impossible
to orchestrate; this natural, unfractured peace, its tiny
temporal life immeasurable, its sparse moment generative,
not taking from me minute by minute, piece by broken piece.

This stillness is not crowded out by fear, desire, loss, or pain.
It is a space where the trees lean away instead of in,
yet still seem to hold (contain) and forgive all human frailty.
Sunlight breaks through the branches, refracting birdlike

shadows on the merciful snow, and I drift down to my knees
telling myself I am less bad for having noticed my deficits.
The forest seems to pause its breath, then blesses me
with confetti of powdered snow and—my God—it's amazing!

Silverskin

Remember the paper herrings I thought you snip-snipped at those first endless hours of polar night?
You: cross-legged on a sooty stump, knit tight in shawl, a headscarf, that wet-hemmed skirt.
Offcuts fell from the blur of your quicksilver fingers: something spangled, danced,
something glittered, luring its blues from the midnight sun. I saw scales on your rivelled hands,
racks of reeking fish flayed for drying in the salted air, icy driftnets stiff as fences.
I'd come to you numb, dumb, stuttering, all my faith fettered to a reticent reindeer; come lost,
bewildered, not knowing if I lived or loved or loathed until you untethered me, took me in-
to your hut (that miserable hut) its sunken roof icicles touching the snow, the doorway so low
we crawled beneath its creaking lintel. You fed the leaping fire, for I was biting cold and hungry
for your milkcaps, eggbutter, wilted scallions. Feeling faint as I glimpsed the ancient blades
displayed above your makeshift bed, you caught me before I fell. Your touch? It felt like papercuts,
despite how ever-so-gently you loosed me from my rabbit-skin boots, filled them with long cut grasses,
upended them under the stove as my eyelids started to droop and I was sinking—sinking—sunk.

❧

Ice chimes woke me. At first, I thought it was the brittle fish smoking in the rafters, sloughing their silvers to gold in the afterglow of a fire dying. But it was the music of your necklace as you tended me; the skeleton of a fingerling (tail curled slightly to the left), its silver-dipped bones rattling me from child-deep sleep to wonder who had crafted it? Who had loved you, got close to the scent of your juniper berry skin? You showed me your silver darlings: a keg of herrings floating in a rose brine of their own diluted blood. One by one, you severed the heads and tails, then holding me by the thumbs, guided them deep inside to spread the flesh apart. Opened, I helped you tear out the whiskery spines, a cranberry red staining each core. Together we spilled slick guts, tugged out the caviar, trimmed the fins, and fried them silverskin-up and sputtering. We ate wordless: all flicker-lit eyes, sucks, slurps and spat bones. Pondering my fearful smile, you took a page of parched stockfish, a charcoal stick from cooling clinker, and scratched a message to your sister in hidden glyphs. You tucked it in my parka pocket, but I didn't want to leave. I wanted you to hook me back by that undecipherable light in your Baltic eyes, the one that makes my belly flip, remember?

[73]

Winterlight

Afterwards, I bathed in winterlight,
lolling in her copper tub, my eyes

raised high to the blackened smoke-
hole grasping the last of my spirit's

wanderings. I soaked until bloated
stars shrank back to invisibility,

and a woozy sun lumbered above
the horizon to spread pale fingers

between birchbark cups of buttermilk,
cloudberries, runes. I curled myself

by her stove, finger-combed my drying
hair, every so often lifting the *láávu's*

flap to watch her scry the ice, and listen
to her frosted lips lasso those ancient

notes around her herd of milky reindeer
feeding on lichen, spruce, fistfuls of salt.

*láávu – a tipi-like nomadic dwelling used by the indigenous people of
Sápmi.*

PART SEVEN

either
THE SNOW QUEEN'S PALACE

or
ICE

Where the novice is considered dead, he is resurrected and taught how to live, but differently than in childhood.

—ARNOLD VAN GENNEP, *The Rites of Passage*

Sixteen Winters

> Better not to have had thee than thus to want thee.
> —*The Winter's Tale* (Act IV, Scene ii)

Mother—stone—hoarfrost.
Each unsafe lune of the lost years

spent traipsing this wasted land
cheerless, weather-bitten

musing only on meeting noses
leaning cheek-to-cheek

with another who lives to love me
swaddle me in woman's flesh.

Shuddering through febrile sleep
the same revolving dream: a statue queen,

winter flowers at her feet, eyes—skin—lips
all warm as she reaches out to touch me,

her treasure. My waking heart dances
but not for joy, not joy.

Alone in this garland, this mirror,
the world, tell me: who will hold me? Who?

Crowberries

More north than this, beyond the fells,
the forests and that abandoned nickel mine
I dream us at the edge of a deep
pink ravine to witness its would-be-crowberries.
Somewhere close, a rushing frothing river,
the full force of it thundering my unsung body.

Undefended, you drift toward sleep.
So, I tiptoe over to a creaking, sun-bleached chute
and feel helpless beside its small, dammed
channel—choked and unable to move.
I am frozen there when you wake and pad back
to me, all language logjammed in my throat.

You hold me from behind, lift my hair
and kiss me at the warm place there,
offering me once more the soft chirr of your birdcall:
oriole—redpoll—the rusty whistle of bullfinch.
Unforgotten Robbergirl, I regret how I crept
away from you. And I miss those old detonations.

Lost Boys

after 'Lux Perpetua Luceat Eis', (1922) by Kathleen Scott

One arm dropped over the edge of the bed, one leg was arched,
and the unfinished part of his laugh was stranded on his mouth,
which was open, showing the little pearls.

—J. M. BARRIE, *Peter Pan*

I go into his room to wake him—my teenage boy—lost
to sleep: arms thrown above his head, legs spread,
neck exposed as if in surrender.
I long to press my nose to the soft fuzz on his cheek,
inhale his warm scent of musk, of sweat, of terror.
But there is nothing I can take from him, nothing I can keep.
I imagine I am the same as any other mother
treading a barefoot requiem from a son I must let go of,
the boy he was—so briefly—already ceasing to be.

In recent weeks, I've noticed how he sizes up to his father,
chest puffed to cockiness, ready to rage over politics, food, me.
Am I meant to intervene or let them fight it out?
I surrender to silences, and inside them hope
he never outgrows us, that eternal light shines on him, always.
I find I too want to sculpt a memorial to this fleeting phase
between boy and not-yet-man, cast it in bronze,
or something else enduring, make it staggeringly beautiful,
a woman's tribute to a youth that's doomed to vanish.

Percy, Sleeping

Visiting you in hospital, those first stunned nights of misty November—when the scent of pumpkin pie couldn't raise you, when your siblings couldn't rattle you, when your father's voice couldn't carry you home—I realised I'd never seen you still before: still and silent and blissful as a baby, your far away smile heavy with sleep. I dreamed you back to the beech woods, thrashing a muddy stick at that shaggy gold dog that tried to snaffle at our picnic. How you curled your lip, bared your teeth, and growled like a wild thing, before chasing it deep into thickets. Afterward, the scent of hounding making you howl, you hunted your chuckling mother who fled from you purposely slow, both of you sensing a primal rule: no parent should outrun their child. You landed panting beside me, so intent on guzzling your carton of warm juice you didn't even notice yourself lolling against my leg, or how much I liked having you there. Lost boy, if only we could whistle you back from Neverland, see you hurtle towards us in your green cap, try to catch you, and miss, as you speed past us hollering and zigzagging between trees. We may no longer be able to hold you, to play with you, but if we close our eyes, we can see you parting the lines of this poem like branches and peeking back at us with your chocolate button eyes, that mop of tufty hair, your flushed, dusty face grinning at us puckishly.

The Spiders of Bear Island

Picture them, white as chalky pods woven inside sleeping
sacks and tucked unseen between two perished slats
of a whaler's hut. I hatched them back to life one night,
stirring from arctic dreams, waking numb, stunned,
limb-frozen, shaking out leg after leg after wiry leg.
I fancied them slip into eight itsy clogs, circumnavigate
each other, leaving a spiral of powdery prints facing north.

Two hundred miles from Spitsbergen, spiders aren't white
at all, but an old blood brown, their abdomens blown
to a juicy shine of fine hairs, black as silver.
How do they endure the vicious winds? Each home a fragile
doily spun more from absence than matter; more hope
than refuge. Like the makeshift put-up of the explorers
who tried to master the arctic in a hot air balloon,
taking no objects fit for a wintering: just penguin suits, tents,
a collapsible boat. Think of them shuddering the brutal
icefields, battling hunger, terror, shattered prayers.

Think of them attempting to rig bewildered minds back
to their mothers' plump eiderdowns; a lover's tender neck;
sun-warm blackberries fed to unblistered lips. Generations
later, bite-scarred bones, a tatty journal, rolls of cracked
celluloid all come to light when their camp resurfaces
with snowmelt. The spiders don't know their luck:
how the natural cryogenics of Bear Island still them in time;
thaw them each spring, as though winter were a bitter dream.

Pulse

The far reaches
of my being—myself
or any sense of it—
are disturbed
by waves of light
emitting from an old
familiar source,
its fragile pulse
strobing from a dark-
distant corner,
a presence sensed,
or felt—taut as a spring—
watching me,
ravenous
for something
I have—or
believe I have—
something alive
enough to reach for;
to reach for
from under the ice.

Eternity Unlocked

The whole room seemed to trickle and weep
with these falling drops in the half dark.
—TARJEI VESAAS, *The Ice Palace*

Here he is, Kai: resurfacing from his deepest freeze,
a latent warmth pinking him as he tugs himself from death-

like sleep. He blinks at me, he cries, lets the wicked
splinter run from his eye. I kneel to hold him,

and see again the mirror (no longer broken), just my own
complete reflection, so long lost, all I can do is kiss it.

As I pull back from this union—our flushed, stunned
faces—pieces of ice rearrange themselves to form a bridge,

a link, the key for our release. As we contemplate escaping
this bitter place, the palace begins to crack, its chandeliers

shattering; its howling corridors crumbling to dust.
Such intense tremors shake my woken bones

with a devotional knowing who it is I must hold onto.
This journey isn't over, I must run back

for her—the Robbergirl—return what I stole, then surrender
to what she stole from me. By which I mean: my heart.

Notes

Ten of these poems were included in 'The Snow Queen Retold', a text and textiles exhibition, produced in collaboration with costume designer Lindsey Holmes, and hosted by The Polar Museum, Cambridge in 2013. | 'White on White' was commissioned by the Polar Museum, Cambridge as part of their 'The Thing Is . . .' exhibition in 2014. | The epigraph for 'Room' is borrowed from Ali Smith's A Woof of One's Own, the inaugural Room of One's Own Lecture in collaboration with Cambridge Literary Festival at Newnham College, Cambridge, 23rd April 2023. | 'Citadel of Salt' was first published in Raceme. | 'Come Home' was first published in Mint: An Anthology of New Writing from ARU (Ed. Penny Hancock, 2015). | The epigraph for 'Sleepless in Nyhavn - II' translates as 'Let me doze off close to your heart', and is from a short story called 'The Dying Child' by Hans Christian Andersen | 'Waterbodies' was first published in River Cam Erasures (Ed. Alice Willitts, 2021) in support of Friends of the River Cam, and produced by erasing some of the foreword to Anglian Water's Pollution Incident Plan 2020–2025 by the CEO of Anglian Water. The original text can be accessed here: bit.ly/3E6fcoZ

'A Forest Opera' was commissioned by The Fitzwilliam Museum, Cambridge in 2023, as part of their 'Dance with the Museum' project and written in response to 'The Dyke' (1865), by Jean-Baptiste-Camille Corot. The poem collages words, phrases, and lines transcribed from project participants as they discussed the painting. | 'Fool's Gold' collages lines and phrases from Macbeth. The poem was commissioned by artist Tom de Freston and first published in The Charnel House

(Bridgedoor Press, 2014). | 'Undiscovered Country' collages lines and phrases from Hamlet. | 'The Suspended Forest' was commissioned by Cambridge Curiosity and Imagination in 2021. It collages lines and phrases transcribed from tree stories by people from across Cambridge during lockdown, 2020. Each story was sparked by a hanging from CCI's Fantastical Forest collection. This ever-growing forest of hangings is displayed each year to mark Tree Charter Day and was recently marched to Westminster as part of Earth Day 2023 protests. | 'Homelands' was written for the Nordic Poetry Festival in 2019, where I collaborated with Sámi poet, Inger-Mari Aikio. | 'Silverskin' was longlisted in the Yeovil Literary Prize in 2015. It was also featured on Fraser Grace's blog The Word Cage in 2020. | 'Winterlight' is dedicated to Naomi Chapman. | 'Lapland Summer' is a translation of Eino Leino's 'Lapin Kesä'. The original poem was a commissioned work for the 1902 annual party of the Ostrobothnia nation: an association for Helsinki University students from Lapland, Oulu, and Vaasa regions. It was intended to reflect their 'homelands' up in the North, in a much wider area than what is now known as Sápmi, which refers only to the very top of the Fennoskandia region, where the Sámi currently live. My translation was commissioned by the Finnish Cultural Foundation in 2019, and is dedicated to Dr. Saara Koikkalainen, who helped with the research trip and translation. | 'The Spiders of Bear Island' is dedicated to Naomi Boneham. | 'Percy, Sleeping' is dedicated to Helen and Thomas Hayes | 'Sixteen Winters' collages lines and phrases from The Winter's Tale.

Acknowledgements

Enormous thanks to Lucy Sheerman, formerly of Arts Council England, who guided my application for the grant that changed my life and enabled my research trips to Denmark and Lapland. To the Finnish Cultural Foundation for commissioning me to translate 'Lapin Kesä', an honour. And to the Society of Authors who funded my family's travel expenses to Finland in 2019 so that I could show my children a country I love.

My thanks to Jen Campbell who edited this collection with care and insight, to Chris Hamilton-Emery who endured every delay on the manuscript with remarkably good humour, and to my agent, Rosie Pierce at Curtis Brown, who repeatedly agreed to me taking time away from my novel to attend to my poetry.

My gratitude to Heather Lane and Sophie Weeks, both formerly of The Polar Museum in Cambridge, who agreed to host me as their Invited Poet while I researched and wrote this collection. I am grateful also to the friends I made both there, and at the Scott Polar Research Institute: Naomi Chapman, Rosie Amos, Willow Silvani, Naomi Boneham, Sophie Rowe, Gareth Rees, Joe Minden, George Cronin, Martin French, Bridget Cusack, Lucy Martin, John Ash, Peter Lund, and Frankie Marsh.

Kiitos! to my Finnish friends for their encouragement and help. To Justiina Dahl for putting me in touch with the Koikkalainen family who welcomed me into their snowy home. To Tuomi-Tuulia Ervasti for driving me into the forest during a blizzard to watch reindeer herders in the Poikajärvi Co-operative at work. To Pälvi Rantala, Hannu Paloniemi, and Johanna Luoma-Aho for the insights into Finnish culture, history, and literature. To Inger-Mari Aikio for my first Sámi lesson. And to Suvi Pilvi King for the subsequent Sámi lessons throughout the first lockdown.

Thank you to the fellow writers who I chat with along the way: to Michael Bayley for his eagle eye, to Megan Hunter and Bec Sollom for brilliant book talks, to Kate Swindlehurst for the happiest research trip to Denmark, to Nancy Campbell and Rebecca Goss for years of correspondence and friendship, and to past and present members of my poetry workshop: Jane Monson, Joanne Limburg, Lucy Hamilton, Stav Poleg, Lucy Sheerman, and in memory of the much-missed Clare Crowther.

To my Swimsisters: Annie, Vanessa, Rosie, Ditty, Jaana and Jane, who brave the icy river with me most days of the year, thank you for your gentle presences in my life.

To Mary, wisest of women, who has been beside me all the way, thank you, always, ('Silverskin' is for you).

Lastly, thanks to my family (near and far, blood ties or none), who generously let me take the time I need to write, I love you. This collection is dedicated to the memory of my daft, affable, chicken-dancing dad, who bought me a copy of *The Snow Queen* on a business trip in Denmark when I was seven. I adored the Robbergirl instantly, she has lived in me ever since.

This book has been typeset by
SALT PUBLISHING LIMITED
using Sabon, a font designed by Jan Tschichold
for the D. Stempel AG, Linotype and Monotype Foundries.
It is manufactured using Holmen Book Cream 70gsm,
a Forest Stewardship Council™ certified paper from the
Hallsta Paper Mill in Sweden. It was printed and bound
by Clays Limited in Bungay, Suffolk, Great Britain.

SHEFFIELD
GREAT BRITAIN
MMXXIII